Petting Zoo

Gail Tuchman

SCHOLASTIC INC.

New York   Toronto   London   Auckland
Sydney   Mexico City   New Delhi   Hong Kong

Read more! Do more!

After you read this book, download your free all-new digital activities.

LEVEL 1

SCHOLASTIC discover more readers

petting zoo

reading fun

enter →

For Mac and PC

ADMIT ONE
389002
389002
389002

You can show what a great reader you are!

Petting zoo counting
Click on the correct numbers.

DISCOVER MORE click

BACK TO THE START home

How many calves are there?	How many animals wallow in mud?	How many animals have webbed feet?	How many animals lay eggs?	How many animals are there in total?
4 2 3	2 7 4	7 3 8	6 8 10	16 20 18

Take quizzes about
the fun facts in this book!

Make some finger puppets!

Choose your favorite animal
from the petting zoo to make.

SCREEN BEFORE back

BACK TO THE START home

You will need . . .

A pencil
Thin white card

Markers, crayons, or
paints and a paintbrush

Scissors

A glue stick

Duck   Chicken   Goat   Pony   Sheep   Cow   Pig   Guinea pig   Alpaca

w click
e numbers . . .

1 2 3 4 5

Play petting zoo games and
activities with videos and sounds!

Log on to
www.scholastic.com/discovermore/readers
Enter this special code: **L16DTMFN4TK1**

BAA! CLUCK! MOO!
The animals are calling.
They're calling to you.

GOATS

SHEEP

BUNNIES

Come see
the animals.

PONIES

COWS

ALPACAS

REMEMBER TO:

Pick up
a map!

Wash your
hands!

DUCKS

PIGS

Come feed them at
the petting zoo.

CHICKENS

GUINEA PIGS

Goats play together.
Kids can climb and jump.
Some goats can leap
over small fences!

Goats are smart. Some
can even open gates.

Billy
(male goat)

Nanny
(female goat)

Kid
(young goat)

7

Goats check
out new things.
They sniff and
nibble them.

Hay

Good food for goats

oats plants  grass corn

Maybe the new
thing is food!
Goats spend half
their time eating.

HOLD A GOAT CAREFULLY.

Sheep get haircuts, like you do. A sheep's coat is called a fleece. It needs to be sheared, or cut, every spring.

Shearing doesn't hurt the sheep.

GIVE MILK TO A LAMB.

Fleece is turned into yarn.

Fleece

Yarn

Yarn is turned into clothes.

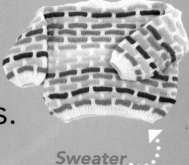

Sweater

11

Bunnies do something called binkying.

They jump up into the air.

BRUSH A BUNNY

Then they
twist and kick
their feet.

Alpacas
hum.
Listen
closely.

They hum
softly
to one
another.

Wild alpacas live
on mountains.
They are in the
camel family.

North
America

South
America

Wild alpacas live
in South America.

**Wild alpaca
herd**

An alpaca
will cry if
there is danger.

TOUCH AN ALPACA'S SOFT HAIR.

Webbed feet
work like
paddles. They
help ducks
swim well in
the water.

HOLD DUCKLINGS GENTLY.

A duck moves from side to side as it walks. This is because of its webbed feet.

Piglets grow fast. They weigh about 2 pounds at birth. In 6 months, they may be 200 pounds!

STROKE A PIGLET.

A mother pig
gives milk
to her piglets.

Guinea pigs
weigh about
2 pounds.
They are
not in the
pig family!

SNUGGLE A GUINEA PIG.

19

Pigs can't sweat to cool down.
Pigs wallow, or roll around
in wet mud.

NEW WORD

wallow
WAH-loh
Pigs **wallow**
in mud on
hot days.

SAY IT OUT LOUD

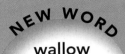

MUD FACTOR 50

The mud helps
stop sunburn.
It also keeps
bugs off pigs.

Animals that wallow

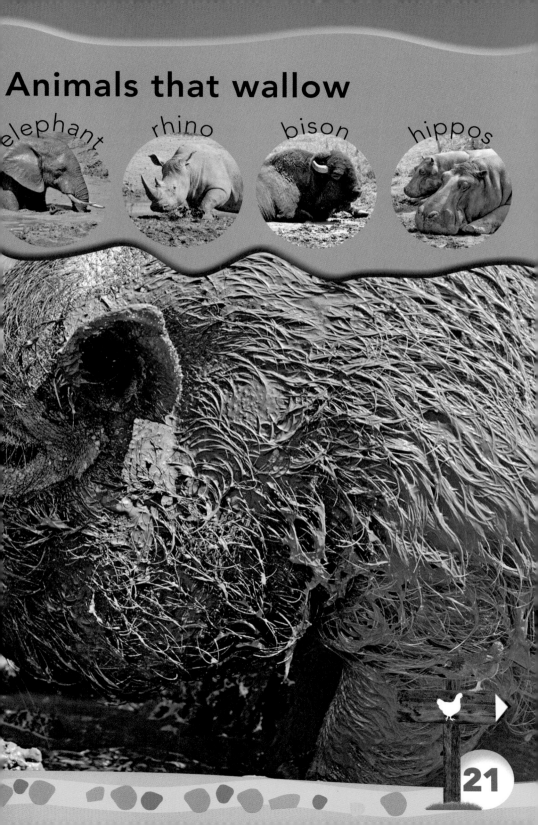

elephant   rhino   bison   hippos

A hen can lay an egg almost every day. She sits on her eggs to keep them warm. The eggs will hatch into chicks.

All birds hatch from eggs.

 Quail Robin Chicken Duck

Chicken

Chick

Chicks grow up to be chickens.

Egg

Hatching

Penguin   Goose   Emu   Ostrich

Chickens have combs on their heads. Combs come in lots of shapes.

Comb

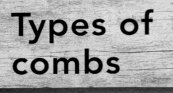

FEED A CHICKEN CORN.

Types of combs

Single   Rose

Chickens have wattles on their heads. These keep them cool.

NEW WORD

wattle

WAH-tuhl

Turkeys can also have **wattles** on their heads.

SAY IT OUT LOUD

Wattle

| Pea | V-shaped | Walnut |

PET A CALF

A baby cow is called a calf.

Calf

Cow

Dr. Cathe and Dr. Nick are vets. They helped a calf.

DR. CATHE AND DR. NICK

Little Nicky
"The calf was very weak. We wrapped him in our jackets. We put him under a heat lamp to keep him warm. It worked! He stood up the next day."

Little Nicky

Before you leave, how about a ride on this pony? Your family can take pictures.

Saddle . . . . ▸

Ponies and horses are different. Ponies are usually smaller.

What a great day at the petting zoo!

Ride a pony.

Pet a bunny.

Hold a chick.

Say hello to a goat.

Feed a piglet.

exit ▶

Glossary

comb
The colorful piece of skin on top of a chicken's head.

fleece
The soft, woolly coat of a sheep.

hatch
To be born by breaking out of an egg.

herd
A large group of animals.

nibble
To eat something by taking small bites.

shear
To cut the hair or wool off a sheep or other animal.

vet
A doctor who treats sick or hurt animals.

wallow
To roll around in mud or water.

wattle
The fold of skin under the head or neck of a chicken, turkey, or other bird.

webbed
Having toes that are connected by folds of skin.

Index

Remember to wash your hands after petting an animal.

Disclaimer: This book is not intended for instruction. Adult supervision and best judgment should always be used when interacting with animals. Be sure to follow all rules when visiting a petting zoo.

ISBN (Trade) 978-0-545-63631-5
ISBN (Clubs) 978-0-545-66124-9

12 11 10 9 8 7 6 5 4 3 2 1   13 14 15 16 17 18/0

Printed in the U.S.A.   40
This edition first printing, December 2013

Scholastic is constantly working to lessen the environmental
impact of our manufacturing processes. To view our
industry-leading paper procurement policy,
visit www.scholastic.com/paperpolicy.

For their generosity of time in sharing their veterinary passion and expertise,
special thanks to Drs. Cathe Montesano and Nick Tallarico.
Thank you also to the petting zoo at DuBois Farms.

Image credits

Photography and artwork

1: iStockphoto/Thinkstock; 2 (chicks tl): cornelia_anghel/Fotolia; 2 (chick tr): nicolesy/iStockphoto; 2 (computer monitor): skodonnell/iStockphoto; 2 (tickets): laurent gendre/Fotolia; 2 (duckling): Lindamstyle/Dreamstime; 2 (chicken): Giuseppe Lancia/Dreamstime; 2 (fence, used throughout): Levkr/Dreamstime; 2 (alpacas): iStockphoto/Thinkstock; 3 (arrows): pagadesign/iStockphoto; 3 (piglet): GlobalP/iStockphoto; 4–5 (inset grass background, used throughout): Satel22/Dreamstime; 4 (goat t): ksena32/Fotolia; 4 (standing lamb): JMichl/iStockphoto; 4 (sitting lamb): Hemera/Thinkstock; 4 (sheep): iStockphoto/Thinkstock; 4 (bunny): Konstantin Yolshin/Shutterstock; 4 (goat b): ksena32/Fotolia; 4 (pony): Elena Titarenco/Dreamstime; 4 (cows): PerfectLazybones/Fotolia; 4 (guinea pig): Vasily77/Dreamstime; 4 (signpost, used throughout): Photka/Dreamstime; 4 (icons l to r): Guilu/Dreamstime, Sergey Yakovlev/Dreamstime, Tribalium/Dreamstime, Roughcollie/Dreamstime; 5 (map): Yin21205/Dreamstime; 5 (handwashing icon): Tribalium/Dreamstime; 5 (alpaca tl): James Brey/iStockphoto; 5 (ducklings): Isselee/Dreamstime, Cristian Baitg/iStockphoto, jarenwicklund/iStockphoto; 5 (white duck): Vasyl Helevachuk/Dreamstime; 5 (pig): GlobalP/iStockphoto; 5 (chicken): Giuseppe Lancia/Dreamstime; 5 (chicks): Sunnybeach/iStockphoto; 5 (guinea pigs): Gerritgr/Fotolia; 5 (alpaca br): Marie-T/iStockphoto; 5 (duckling bl): Chepko/iStockphoto; 6–7 (sky, grass, used throughout): Tatyana Vychegzhanina/Dreamstime; 6 (goat cl): Isselee/Dreamstime; 7 (goat tl): GlobalP/iStockphoto; 7 (billy): Iakov Filimonov/Dreamstime; 7 (nanny): Andygaylor/Dreamstime; 7 (kid b): Snickerdoodle Photography/iStockphoto; 7 (gate b): Amandamhanna/Dreamstime; 7 (latch): Soundsnaps/Dreamstime; 6–7 (all others): Penny Lamprell/Scholastic Inc.; 8 (goat, hay): Martijn Mulder/Dreamstime; 8 (wood background): Pedro2009/Dreamstime; 8bl: Christian Jung/Dreamstime; 8bcl: Kulikova/Dreamstime; 8bcr: Ahmet Gündoan/Dreamstime; 8br: Peter Zijlstra/Dreamstime; 9 (goat l): Tanawaty/Dreamstime; 9 (goat r, background): ACMPhoto/iStockphoto; 9 (hay b): Kelpfish/Dreamstime; 9 (hand icon, used throughout): Samuvel/Dreamstime; 9 (sheep icon): Guilu/Dreamstime; 9 (grass below signpost, used throughout): Skalapendra/Dreamstime; 9 (lamb): GlobalP/iStockphoto; 10: GoodOlga/iStockphoto; 11tc: Grigorios Moraitis/iStockphoto; 11 (inset): Robert Wisdom/Dreamstime; 11 (fleece): esemelwe/iStockphoto; 11cl: shirhan/iStockphoto; 11 (sweater): BVDC/iStockphoto; 11 (bunny icon): Roughcollie/Dreamstime; 11 (bunny): Isselee/Dreamstime; 12 (white bunny tl): Duncan Noakes/Dreamstime; 12 (mother, baby tl): Isselee/Dreamstime; 12–13 (red wood b): Tombaky/Dreamstime; 12–13 (straw b): Kelpfish/Dreamstime; 12 (large brown bunny): Penny Lamprell/Scholastic Inc.; 12 (inset): Penny Lamprell/Scholastic Inc.; 12–13 (leaping bunny): George Caswell/Getty Images; 13 (alpaca icon): Lantapix/Dreamstime; 13 (brown bunny r): Rubberball/Mike Kemp/Getty Images; 14: Alison Williams/Dreamstime; 15 (sky): Elena Elisseeva/Dreamstime; 15tl: Zoom-zoom/Dreamstime; 15 (map): Adamgibson/Dreamstime; 15 (landscape): jeantrekkeur/Fotolia; 15 (alpaca herd): Christian Larue/Fotolia; 15 (inset): Levranii/Dreamstime; 15 (duck icon): Sergey Yakovlev/Dreamstime; 15 (ducklings): Stefan Andronache/Dreamstime; 16 (ducklings, duck l): Thierry Vialard/Dreamstime, GlobalP/iStockphoto, Danil Chepko/Dreamstime; 16 (inset): Penny Lamprell/Scholastic Inc.; 16 (main duckling): Photowitch/Dreamstime; 16–17 (green reeds): Tommason/Dreamstime; 16–17 (water): Melissa King/Dreamstime; 17 (l ducklings t to b): vusta/Dreamstime, Studio-Annika/iStockphoto, GlobalP/iStockphoto, JodiJacobson/iStockphoto, Anatolii/Fotolia; 17 (white ducks): Penny Lamprell/Scholastic Inc.; 17 (pond t): Leelloo/Dreamstime; 17 (duckling tr): Olga Yastremska/Dreamstime; 17 (pig icon): Batagaja/Dreamstime; 17 (pig): Miiicha/iStockphoto; 18–19 (straw background): Edward Westmacott/iStockphoto; 18 (pigs): janecat/iStockphoto; 19 (inset tr): Image_Source_/iStockphoto; 19 (pig family): Susan Sheldon/Dreamstime; 19 (straw c): Nito100/Dreamstime; 19 (red wood): Tombaky/Dreamstime; 19 (green wood): nataliazakharova/Fotolia; 19 (guinea pig l): Alptraum/Dreamstime; 19 (guinea pigs c): Simone Van Der Berg/Dreamstime; 19 (guinea pig r): GlobalP/iStockphoto; 19 (inset b): Penny Lamprell/Scholastic Inc.; 20–21 (main image): Eduard Kyslynskyy/Dreamstime; 20 (mud splatters): Roberto Pirola/Dreamstime; 20 (sunscreen): ARSELA/iStockphoto; 20tl: Michael Sheehan/Dreamstime; 21tcl: Stu Porter/Dreamstime; 21tcr: jlandrow/iStockphoto; 21tr: gennaro coretti/Fotolia; 21 (chicken): Sval77/Dreamstime; 21 (chicken icon): Tribalium/Dreamstime; 22 (background): nataliazakharova/Fotolia; 22 (hen, nest): thieury/Shutterstock; 22 (quail egg): Lepas/Dreamstime; 22 (quail): Boobathy/Dreamstime; 22 (robin egg): Linda Yolanda/iStockphoto; 22 (robin): Pperegrim/Dreamstime; 22 (chicken egg): Chris Leachman/Dreamstime; 22 (chicken): Anatolii/Fotolia; 22 (duck egg): Kooslin/Dreamstime; 22 (duck): Linda Steward/iStockphoto; 23 (chick): Photowitch/Dreamstime; 23 (egg tr): Chris Leachman/Dreamstime; 23 (hatching chick, egg): Photowitch/Dreamstime; 23 (penguin egg, penguin): Isselee/Dreamstime; 23 (goose egg): Vasyl Helevachuk/Dreamstime; 23 (goose): Sean Nel/Dreamstime; 23 (emu egg): dovate/iStockphoto; 23 (emu): GlobalP/iStockphoto; 23 (ostrich egg): ayala_studio/iStockphoto; 23 (ostrich): vblinov/iStockphoto; 24 (inset): SKLA/iStockphoto; 24 (chicken tr): panbazil/Shutterstock; 24–25 (roof): Penny Lamprell/Scholastic Inc.; 24–25 (green wood): nataliazakharova/Fotolia; 24 (gray wood): enviromantic/iStockphoto; 24–25 (brown wood): Dreamstimepoint/Dreamstime; 24bc: panbazil/Shutterstock; 24br: Isselee/Dreamstime; 25 (cow icon): Darrenw/Dreamstime; 25 (calf): JMichl/iStockphoto; 25 (chicken tl, chick): panbazil/Shutterstock; 25bl: Isselee/Dreamstime; 25bc: Ammit Jack/Shutterstock; 25br: Margojh/Dreamstime; 26–27 (background): Pedro2009/Dreamstime; 26 (inset): emholk/iStockphoto; 26–27 (main): Dr. Ajay Kumar Singh/Dreamstime; 27 (inset): Drs. Cathe and Nick Tallarico; 27 (shed): patty_c/iStockphoto; 27 (Little Nicky): Drs. Cathe and Nick Tallarico; 27 (pony icon): Roughcollie/Dreamstime; 28–29 (bushes, white fence): Johannesk/Dreamstime; 28–29 (main image): Elena Titarenco/Dreamstime; 28 (gate b): jorgesa/Dreamstime; 28 (gray wood): enviromantic/iStockphoto; 29 (ride a pony): Elena Titarenco/Dreamstime; 29 (bunny): Pavla Zakova/Dreamstime; 29 (chick): hartcreations/iStockphoto; 29 (goat): xiao-ming/iStockphoto; 29 (piglet): SchulteProductions/iStockphoto; 30–31 (main image): Tanawaty/Dreamstime; 31 (handwashing icon): Tribalium/Dreamstime; 31 (duckling): Art_man/Fotolia; 32 (bunnies): camellias/Fotolia; 32 (meadow): Monika3stepsahead/Dreamstime; 32 (duckling): jarenwicklund/iStockphoto; 32 (pig): GlobalP/iStockphoto; all others: Scholastic Inc.

Cover
Front cover: (sheep icon) Oorka/Dreamstime; (rooster icon) Talisalex/Dreamstime; (goat icon) Oorka/Dreamstime; (bunny icon) Ashestos/Dreamstime; (donkey icon) Oorka/Dreamstime; (duck icon) Lantapix/Dreamstime; (trees) Nikada/iStockphoto; (bl) Belkin & Co/Fotolia; (br) Farinoza/Fotolia; (grass) narvikk/iStockphoto. Back cover: (tr) GlobalP/iStockphoto; (computer monitor) Manaemedia/Dreamstime. Inside front cover: (ducks) Thomas Seybold/iStockphoto; (br) Yakovliev/iStockphoto.